# Cornucopia

# Cornucopia.

## by Robert S. Oliver.

DRAWINGS BY FREDERICK HENRY BELLI

*Atheneum · New York · 1978*

LIBRARY OF CONGRESS CATALOGING IN PUBLICATION DATA

Oliver, Robert S   Cornucopia.

1. Children's poetry.   I. Title.
PN6110.C40517      811'.5'4      77-24655
ISBN 0-689-30626-1


Copyright © 1978 by Robert S. Oliver
All rights reserved
Published simultaneously in Canada by
McClelland & Stewart, Ltd.
Manufactured in the United States by
The Book Press, Brattleboro, Vermont
*designed by Mary M. Ahern*
First Edition

*To Ginny, Rich, and John*

# Contents

# Cornucopia

# Ants

This morning at five I awoke with a cough;
I needed a lozenge to turn the thing off.
I reached in the cupboard, with scarcely a glance,
And there in the cough drops were three hundred ants!

A train of them ran down the wall to the floor,
Along by the baseboard and under the door,
And then by the carpet, the length of the hall,
And out through a very small hole in the wall.

I looked on a shelf and found bug-killer aid,
And all 'round their entrance judiciously sprayed.
And then with a sponge, and a great deal of strain,
I washed ev'ry one of them right down the drain.

So that ends my tale but does not end my plight—
I'm wondering where I shall find them tonight.

# Bees

Stop, and be
Still, honey,
Listen to the
Sound.

What is the
Drone that we're
Hearing all a-
Round?

What can it
Be? Do you
Think it will ex-
Plode?

Black buzzing
Bees by the
Border of the
Road.

# The Cougar

There was once a thin cougar named Sean,
Who had far less of brain than of brawn.
    He would always announce
    His intention to pounce,
But his dinners, by then, would be gone.

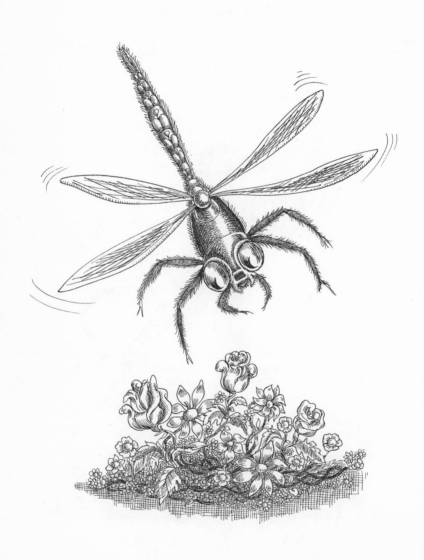

# The Dragonfly

Glassy wings,
A cage of legs,
Bulging eyes,
Mandibles.
A ghastly helicopter
Waiting—

Waiting—


Waiting—



Waiting—

# The Eel

The feel
Of an eel
Is slippery,
Slimy;
He's sleek
And he's black
As a panther
At night.
He slides
Through your fingers
Rapidly,
Slyly;
A flip
Of his tail
And he slips
Out of sight.

# Flamingos

Ah-choo!
(I couldn't help it.)

In a furious flurry
Of flapping, flailing wings
The whole flock took flight
And fled frantically in all directions.

In the center of the silent swamp
I was left alone,
Blowing my nose.

# The Goose

At the end of the train, in the big red caboose,
In a cage, very cross, sat Miranda the goose.
And she asked the conductor, "Sir, why must I stay
In this drafty caboose for the rest of the day?"

The conductor replied, with a sort of a sneer,
"If you don't pay first class, you have got to stay here.
Did you think you could travel to Kalamazoo
With a ticket that cost but a buck twenty-two?"

Poor Miranda remained in her cage, and she thought,
"Well, I guess this is all of the comfort I bought,
And I'm stuck in this chilly caboose for a while—
But the next time I travel, I'll do it in style."

So the lesson Miranda reluctantly learned
Was: "You get what you've paid for,
                    And keep what you've earned."

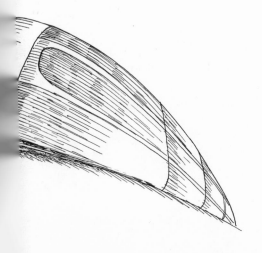

# The Herring

A hard-of-hearing herring thought he heard a haddock say,
"I think the sole and halibut will stay inside today.
The waves are high,
And somehow I
Fear trouble heads our way."

The hard-of-hearing herring wasn't sure he heard it right.
He was a careful creature, though, and kept himself from
        sight.
Now this was wise,
For no surprise
Would cause *that* fish a fright.

No sooner had the herring hid within a crevice dark,
Than what came by marauding but a hammerheaded shark.
It stopped to grab
A tasty crab
That strayed out for a lark.

And then it looked around to find some other fish to greet;
The crab was but a morsel, and it wanted more to eat.
And while it preyed,
The herring stayed
Within his safe retreat.

When finally the shark was gone, the herring left his hole,
And cautiously rejoined his friends, the halibut and sole.
They all agreed
That when sharks feed,
The careless pay the toll.

The moral: when you have a hint of danger, heed your
    hunch.
You live within a world that's filled with jaws that like to
    crunch.
You must beware,
And move with care,
Or you'll be someone's lunch.

# Ichthyosaurus

*(Extinct, fortunately)*

Ye gods and little fishes,
    It's a swimming dinosaur!
He certainly looks vishes,
    And I'm glad he lives no maur.


# J's

Jack rabbit, jackdaw, jaguar,
Jay.
Jellyfish, jewfish, junco,
Jay.
Stellar's jay, blue jay, scrub jay,
Jay.
Fly away,
Far away,
Stay away,
Jay.

# Kangaroo

Kangaroo hopped to the pink tureen
    And ordered a bucket of chowder;
Gurgled it down in a gulp or two
    And called for another one, louder.
"More!" he cried, like Oliver Twist,
    "This soup is so warm and delicious."
Cook replied, "More-soup-ial, eh?"
    And granted the kangaroo's wishes.

# The Lynx

The lynx
Has never seen the sphinx;
The reason is compelling.
The lands
Beset by blowing sands
Are not the lynx's dwelling.

I looked in the Britannica
(Likewise "Americannica")
And nowhere could I find, in all the tedious description,
A note
Or even hint remote
His habitat's Egyptian.

# The Monkey

Mischievous monkey; behavior cantankerous,
Raucous and crude, argumentative, rancorous,
Crafty, deceitful, activities prankerous,
Grabber of food, and you don't even thankerous.

Mischievous monkey, what *are* we to do?
*You* don't like *us*, and we *sure* don't like *you*!

# The Newt

The newt,
To grow,
Begins
To molt,

Until,
When full
Of years,
He's olt.

# The Osprey

Now a hungry young osprey named Lee
Took his catch to the top of a tree,
    And said, "Fifty-foot eels
      Make for very long meals—
That's a big enough dinner for me."

# Ptwo in The Bush

The ptarmigan is
    ptimid, and he
    very seldom
    flies.

The pterodactyl
    was the pterror
    of the ancient
    skies.

# Quinquemaculatus

Five-spotted hawk moth
Drinking from the trumpet vine,
Do you know your name?

# Rabbits

Teaching rabbits how to read is not an easy job;
They just don't seem to concentrate, like Ginny, Rich, or
    Bob.
Johnny knows his A B C's—I'm sure that he will pass;
But all my rabbits think about is running through the grass.

Teaching rabbits how to count is difficult to do;
They just don't have the aptitude, like Fran or Mary Lou.
Heather knows her 1, 2, 3's—I'm sure that she will pass;
But all my rabbits think about is running through the grass.

Teaching rabbits how to spell is such a hopeless chore;
They just don't get the hang of it, like Harold or Lenore.
Jessica spells perfectly—I'm sure that she will pass;
But all my rabbits think about is running through the grass.

Teaching rabbits history's the hardest job of all;
They don't remember Washington, like Eric, Joe, or Paul.
Carroll knows his presidents—I'm sure that he will pass;
But all my rabbits think about is running through the grass.

What to do with rabbits? It really makes me burn.
I just can't teach them anything. They just don't seem to
    learn.
All the others learn so well, I know that they will pass;
But all my rabbits think about is running through the grass.

# The Swallow

An excitable swallow named Will
Was afraid he would always be ill.
    And his fears became true—
    He contracted the flu,
And a migraine, the mumps, and a chill.

# The Toad

In days of old, those far off times
  Of high romance and magic,
A toad was an enchanted prince,
  A transformation tragic.

Today the toad is studied as
  A scientific topic—
No prince is found, although we look
  With vision microscopic.

And yet, the prince is there—he's there
  As clearly as can be.
Forget your microscope, my friend,
  And use your mind to see!

# The Underwing Moth

Search carefully on the trunk of
      this old apple tree.
Down—
And up—
And all around,
And you will find an underwing moth
      quietly resting,
Wings furled,
Scarcely discernible,
Like a piece of brown bark.

Nudge her gently,
And a flash of pink will brighten
    the orchard
When she flies.

# Vampires

The vampire bats all wear bright purple hats,
And I'll tell you the reason they need 'em—
They figure this garb will distract from the barb,
When they puncture their victims to bleed 'em.

# The Weevil

Alfalfa—, Rice—, and especially Boll—, the
Weevil
Is a disaster
Primeval,
A plague
Medieval.

It puts the planters' best laid plans in a state of
Upheaval.
It places their harvests beyond
Retrieval.
It is an unmitigated
Evil.

If only millions of years ago this
Misbegotten
Voracious insect had
Forgotten—
Cotton.

# Xylophagous Insects

All people agree
That the termite is greedy—
A creature
Whose presence makes homeowners frown.
He gobbles with glee;
Whether wealthy or needy
He'll eature
Supports till your home
                    tum-
                        bles
                            down.

# Yellowjackets

Ouch!
Ow!
Oo.

I should have
Known better
Than
To have stuck
My head
Inside
That hollow tree
To see
What
That strange angry
Buzzing noise
Was.

# The Zebu

Although it's hard to understand,
The zebu leads a life that's grand.
He wanders freely through the land.

Although he strays on road and field,
The people reverently yield,
Because of custom long congealed.

Although he need not push nor pull,
His pampered stomach's always full.
It's great when you're a sacred bull.